W9-AEE-931

Artist BIOGRAPHIES

Willem de Kooning

The Life of an Artist

Louise Hawes

Enslow Publishers, Inc.

40 Industrial Road   PO Box 38
Box 398   Aldershot
Berkeley Heights, NJ 07922   Hants GU12 6BP
USA   UK
http://www.enslow.com

Willem de Kooning

Library of Congress Cataloging-in-Publication Data

Hawes, Louise.
    Willem de Kooning : the life of an artist / Louise Hawes.
      p. cm. — (Artist biographies)
    Includes index.
    Summary: Discusses the private and professional life of the twentieth-century American painter who was part of the Abstract Expressionism movement of art.
    ISBN 0-7660-1884-9
    1. De Kooning, Willem, 1904—Juvenile literature. 2. Artists—United States—Biography—Juvenile literature. [1. De Kooning, Willem, 1904- 2. Artists. 3. Painting, American.] I. Title. II. Artist biographies (Berkeley Heights, N.J.)
    N6537.D43 H39 2002
    759.13—dc21

                                    2002011986

Printed in the United States of America

10 9 8 7 6 5 4 3 2 1

To Our Readers: We have done our best to make sure all Internet addresses in this book were active and appropriate when we went to press. However, the author and the publisher have no control over and assume no liability for the material available on those Internet sites or on other Web sites they may link to. Any comments or suggestions can be sent by e-mail to comments@enslow.com or to the address on the back cover.

Illustration Credits: AP/Wide World Photos, pp. 27, 36; Archives of American Art, Smithsonian Institute, pp. 15, 21; The Art Institute of Chicago, p. 25; © Corel Corporation, p. 5; Courtesy of Hackett-Freedman Gallery, San Francisco, p. 31; Digital image © The Museum of Modern Art/Licensed by SCALA/Art Resource, NY, p. 39; Kevin Clarke, p. 33; Library of Congress, p. 9; Linda McCartney © Estate of Linda McCartney, p. 40; National Museum of American Art, Washington, DC/Art Resource, NY, p. 17; *New York Then and Now,* Dover Publications, Inc., 1976, p. 11; Scala/Art Resource, NY, p. 22; Tate Gallery/Art Resource, NY, p. 28.

Cover Illustration: Linda McCartney © Estate of Linda McCartney

Contents

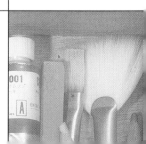

Chapter 1

Cowboy Dreams

As an adult, Willem de Kooning lived up to his last name, which means "the King" in Dutch. He became a world-famous artist, a leader of Action Painting. This was a new kind of art that showed how a painter moved and felt when he worked. Thousands of people saw his work in exhibitions. Critics praised him. His paintings were sold to museums and art lovers around the globe. He was even invited to the White House to receive the Presidential Medal of Freedom.

In America, de Kooning's friends called him Bill. But as a young boy in Holland, he was known as Wim. Born in Rotterdam in 1904,

De Kooning grew up in Rotterdam, Holland, watching ships sail in and out of the harbor. He read American magazines and dreamed of traveling to the United States, the home of Mickey Mouse and Charlie Chaplin.

Wim lived with his mother after his parents divorced. Cornelia de Kooning was a harsh, tough-minded woman who ran a waterfront bar for sailors. She believed the worst of everyone, even her small son. She used to "teach" Wim with slaps and kicks.

Wim dropped out of school when he was only twelve years old. He could not wait to earn enough money to get away from home. All day long he painted hand-lettered signs and decorated store windows. At night, though, Wim dreamed of cowboys, movie stars, and the exciting life he had heard about in America. He was already planning his escape.

Soon Wim's employers noticed that the sturdy, blond boy was not only a hard worker but also very talented. They encouraged him to attend art school. So, for eight years, Wim worked during the day and studied at the Rotterdam Academy of Fine Arts at night.

He planned to earn his living in America with many different skills—carpentry, lettering, furniture repair, and painting. But he never thought about being just a painter. Years later, he laughed when he remembered that he and the other students at the Academy thought painting pictures was only "good for old men with beards."

He changed his mind about that when he went to work, at the age of sixteen, for a large Dutch department store. The store's art director took an interest in Wim. He taught him about the exciting things that modern European artists were doing. He also told him about the designs of a new American architect, Frank Lloyd Wright.

Wim was more determined than ever to get to America. He still loved cowboys and movie stars, but now he had a new American dream. He hoped to find a place where he could experiment with fresh ideas about color and form in art.

A few years after he graduated from the Academy, Wim met some sailors in his mother's bar. They found him a job in the engine room of a freighter sailing to America. When the boat docked in Virginia in August 1926, Wim jumped off.

He had no money, and he knew only one word of English—yes. But Wim pictured cowboys rounding up cattle in the West and skyscrapers and jazz clubs in the East. Surely there was room in this huge, exciting country for a young man who had won prizes in art school.

De Kooning was interested in the work of American architect Frank Lloyd Wright (left), who designed the Guggenheim Museum in New York City.

Chapter 2

New York! New York!

After landing in Virginia, de Kooning boarded other ships and managed to sail all the way up the coast to Hoboken, New Jersey. Hoboken was right across the Hudson River from the biggest, dreamiest American city of them all— New York. For a while, de Kooning worked as a house painter in Hoboken. Here he made American friends. They called him Bill, taught him English, and took him into New York to see movies.

In 1927, de Kooning got the chance to move to an apartment in New York. He was a handsome twenty-three-year-old who loved to talk. He made friends everywhere he

After World War II, New York came to be known as the modern art capital of the world. De Kooning and his artist friends were sometimes known as The New York School.

went. But it was a kitten that introduced him to the world of art!

De Kooning found a small, hungry, black-and-white kitten on a city street and took it home.

One day it climbed onto his fire escape and jumped into the apartment upstairs. Two men shared the apartment; one was a filmmaker, the other a poet. After they had returned his pet, de Kooning's upstairs neighbors took him to meet art critics, painters, writers, ballet dancers, and filmmakers all over the city. De Kooning's new friends were the people who were making American art.

Instead of painting houses, de Kooning began to paint pictures. But he was never satisfied with his colors and shapes. He did not like to sign his paintings because he did not like to finish them. He was sure he could always find ways to make them better.

De Kooning liked to learn from others. Three painters who taught him a lot later became famous artists themselves. Arshile Gorky, Stuart Davis, and

John Graham took de Kooning to museums, showed him their work, and taught him what they had learned. "They knew I had my own eyes," de Kooning said later, "but I wasn't always looking in the right direction. I was certainly in need of a helping hand at times."

In fact, all the painters in New York helped each other. As the 1920s came to a close, the Depression brought hard times to America. Many artists lived in apartments with no heat, refrigerators, telephones, washing machines, or vacuum cleaners. De Kooning left his oven on to stay warm and kept his milk outside on the fire escape in the winter to keep it cold. People loaned each other money, found jobs for each other, and shared what they had.

The government helped too. In 1935, de Kooning found work in a new program designed by President Franklin Roosevelt called the Works Progress Administration (WPA). This program paid de Kooning a weekly salary to do paintings for offices and public buildings. It was not a big salary, but it was enough for him to live on. He never went back to house painting again.

De Kooning did find other painting jobs as well. He painted scenery for ballets, portraits of important New Yorkers, and murals for wealthy homeowners. Once, an art collector asked him to restore a valuable painting he owned. That meant cleaning it up and repainting areas where the paint had faded. De Kooning agreed to try. The painting was a landscape. When de Kooning started cleaning it, he accidentally wiped away some cows that were in the background. He was afraid to tell the painting's owner. He worked for weeks, sketching and sketching until he made cows just like the ones he had wiped away. When he gave the painting back, the collector thanked him and said the picture "looked like new."

De Kooning never cleaned anyone else's paintings again! But he kept cleaning his own. Every morning, he wiped away what he had painted the night before. Every day, he painted over yesterday's painting. He was determined to make his art better and better.

De Kooning was part of a group of New York artists called The Irascibles. He poses here (back row, far left) with the rest of the group for *Life* magazine.

Chapter 3

Painting in Action

People in New York began to talk about the way de Kooning and his new friends painted. They did not try to make what they painted look real. Instead, they used colors and shapes to show how they felt when they painted. This style of painting was called Abstract Expressionism.

De Kooning's paintings showed his feelings and his energy even more than the work of his friends. His paintings were not always totally abstract—sometimes you can recognize objects and people in them. But they were always full of action. He let his brushstrokes and pencil scratches and even bits of paper stay on the

The Wave, 1942–1944. If you are wondering what this is a picture of, forget about it! Focus on the colors, shapes, and energy of the painting instead. This is not old-fashioned painting. This is modern art. You might just think it's crazy. Or you might find that it gives you an interesting feeling that you like.

canvas. He often painted over things or scraped off parts he did not like with a spatula. He wanted people to see how a painting was made, not just stand back and admire a pretty surface.

In 1942, a gallery included de Kooning's work in one of their exhibits. The public liked the energy and excitement they saw. One art critic called this type of painting Action Painting, and the name stuck.

De Kooning used brushes, sandpaper, even pieces of cardboard to push the paint around on his canvases. He liked to keep his canvases wet so he could work on the same painting for days and weeks, sometimes years. "I have to keep my paintings wet for months at a time," he said, "in order to keep them alive."

Lots of visitors came to watch de Kooning work. One of them was a young art student named Elaine Fried. Elaine and de Kooning had long discussions about how and why artists painted. They argued. They laughed. They painted together. They fell in love. In 1943, they married.

Both of them were serious about their art. They worked very hard at painting. Even when they had fun, it was with other painters. They spent all their evenings with their friends, talking about how they wanted to change the way people looked at art. Elaine wrote about their new style of painting for newspapers and magazines. The Action Painters were stirring up the art world. In 1948, Bill de Kooning had his first one-man show, a whole gallery of paintings done just by him.

To get ready for the show, de Kooning bought gallons and gallons of black and white house paint. Because the paint was cheap, he did not have to worry about the cost. Even more important, he knew that without bright colors, the movement of his lines would speak loud and clear. The show was a sensation. It got everyone talking.

The more people talked, the more galleries wanted to show de Kooning's paintings. He had to think of names for all his new work. Sometimes he made up silly titles. One of his abstract paintings is full of jagged patches of color. He called it *Ruth's Zowie* because a woman named Ruth said, "Zowie!" when she saw it. Often he let other people title his paintings, or he simply called them *Untitled*. Naming his work was one more way of

De Kooning spent most of his time in his studio painting. He lived to paint. Here he is in front of one of his many paintings of women.

Untitled, 1944. De Kooning had very good early training as an artist in Holland. He could make things look realistic, but he preferred to show his feelings and his own unique vision. The objects in this painting seem sort of familiar. But the painting gives you a feeling rather than telling you a story.

saying it was done. De Kooning still hated the idea of finishing a painting. He felt he could work on it forever.

De Kooning began making some money from his painting. But it was not enough for a vacation.

Elaine wanted to get out of the city. In 1948, de Kooning took a summer job as an art instructor at a college in the mountains of North Carolina. He was a good teacher, and his students liked him. In between classes, de Kooning worked on a new painting. He called it *Asheville,* after the town the college was in.

This new painting was not black-and-white. De Kooning was using colors again. Created in the clean, crisp air of the mountains, *Asheville* had a bold, open feeling to it. It was the first of many exciting color paintings to come.

Chapter 4

Bill's "Girls"

In 1950 and 1951, de Kooning took another teaching job, this time at Yale University. It was the last time he would teach. Even though he loved working with students, he did not want to spend time away from his easel.

In 1950, de Kooning did a painting called *Excavation,* a piece many critics have called his finest. Like *Asheville,* it combines the movement and energy of his earlier black-and-white paintings with striking bits of color. But color was not the only surprise de Kooning had in store for the New York art world.

In the early 1950s, de Kooning used even brighter colors and more frantic lines to paint

Excavation, 1950. Not all de Kooning's paintings in the 1950s were of women. In *Excavation,* there are no recognizable things or people at all, just space filled with lots of active brushstrokes.

pictures of women. These paintings were not just blotches of colors. They showed women with distorted faces and bodies. The faces were sometimes smiling, sometimes angry.

De Kooning never told people why his women were such fierce giants. For thousands of years, artists had been drawing, painting, and sculpting delicate, beautiful women. De Kooning had chosen to show women in a totally different light. Today some critics think he was poking fun at the traditional way of showing women.

De Kooning called the women in these paintings his "girlies" and said he thought they were cute. Most of the people who crowded into galleries to see them did not agree. Some said the paintings proved de Kooning hated women. Others said the images were too angry.

Once again de Kooning had people talking.

And once again, the more people talked, the more famous he became. Now he could afford expensive paints and a new apartment. Many of his friends were famous artists— Jackson Pollock, Marisol, Robert Motherwell, and Franz Kline. But de Kooning was the most famous of all. He had finally lived up to his Dutch name. He was a king at last—the king of Action Painters.

This is de Kooning in 1968. At age sixty-four, he was both famous and rich. He could afford to buy all the best art supplies and experiment as much as he wanted.

27

Women Singing II, 1966. Can you recognize these two figures as women? They seem to have their arms raised and their mouths wide open. Did you see these things before you looked at the title of the painting?

Even though he was famous and rich, de Kooning still worked hard. His personal life was difficult, though. He and Elaine drifted in and out of each other's lives. Sometimes they were happy as a couple. Sometimes they would fight. And sometimes they would decide to live apart. Their friends worried about them both.

In 1956, de Kooning and a young woman named Joan Ward had a daughter, Lisbeth—Lisa for short. De Kooning and Elaine separated. One day, when Lisa was just two years old, de Kooning walked into his studio to find baby handprints all over one of his paintings. At first he was angry with Lisa. "But," he said, "the more I looked at it, the more I liked it, and I soon realized I couldn't have done better myself." He left the little handprints in the painting, and he named it *Lisbeth's Painting*.

An Artist Whose Work Is Never Done

De Kooning had some rather unusual work habits. Typically he would start his day by scraping the paint off of a canvas he had been working on the day before. This was possible because oil paint takes a while to dry. De Kooning would mix his paints with water and other solvents to make his paint as liquid and as slow-drying as possible. This way he could keep wiping it off and reworking the painting. At night he would cover up his canvases to slow down the drying process even further.

De Kooning was often more interested in getting one particular part of the painting just right—perhaps a person's hand or some wrinkled clothing. He would work and work on that one section and pay little attention to the rest of the painting. Many paintings were declared "finished" only because an art dealer who visited de Kooning hauled the painting out to display or sell it.

Two Women, 1965.

Chapter 5

Back to the Sea

By the 1960s, de Kooning's painting had once again become abstract, which means he did not try to show objects or people that looked realistic. Instead he put great splashes of color and light across his canvases. The horizontal lines of many of these paintings look like sand and sea. Perhaps he was inspired by the beautiful beaches on Long Island, where he and his new family took vacations. Or perhaps he remembered the great ocean off the Dutch coast where he grew up.

But de Kooning had left Holland far behind. On March 13, 1962, he became an American citizen. Making a fresh start, he moved with

This is de Kooning in his studio. He always had many works in progress at the same time.

Joan Ward and their daughter to a new home at the beach.

But de Kooning's lifestyle was still wild. Now that he was a famous artist, he had many invitations to choose from. One of the invitations came from the White House. In 1964, when de Kooning was sixty years old, President Lyndon B. Johnson invited him to Washington, D.C., to accept the Presidential Medal of Freedom. For a year after that, the president continued to invite de Kooning to meet visiting leaders from foreign countries. But in 1965, de Kooning signed a protest against America's war in Vietnam. He was never invited to the White House again.

In the 1970s, everyone wanted to buy a de Kooning painting. De Kooning hired assistants to help him move and store his huge canvases. His paintings sold for higher and higher prices. Sometimes he painted people, especially women. Sometimes he created new abstracts, charged with brighter colors and busier, more nervous brushstrokes than ever before.

On a visit to Japan, de Kooning met the famous Japanese sculptor Isamu Noguchi. He decided to try sculpting, but he did not work in stone, like Noguchi. Instead he used clay. "I liked the way it worked in my hands," he said. "If something didn't look right, I could destroy it and start all over, the way I did with my paintings."

By 1979, de Kooning was drinking too much alcohol and not taking good care of himself. He was seventy-five. He had left his family and was

De Kooning took up sculpture when he was about sixty-five years old. He made this bronze sculpture, called *Standing Figure,* in 1969. Here it is being installed outside a major art museum in Boston. It weighs almost four tons and stands twelve feet high.

living alone. He hardly painted at all. His wife, Elaine, decided to move back in with him and try to get him to stop drinking. That helped de Kooning. Soon he was painting again.

Chapter 6

The Last Paintings

After twenty years of living apart, Elaine and de Kooning were back together. Elaine took charge of his diet, his work, and his friends. During the early 1980s, de Kooning stopped drinking and started living a healthier life. He and Elaine stayed home with their new cat, a beautiful white Angora named Mr. Mongo. They walked on the beach. They ate good meals, and neither of them drank.

When de Kooning began to paint again, his work was less nervous. The colors and

Woman I, 1950-52. De Kooning worked on this painting for two years. It made de Kooning an international celebrity. Some critics didn't like it because they thought it was ugly. Others thought de Kooning was a true genius.

Musician Paul McCartney (left) was inspired by the works of de Kooning (right) to become a painter himself. This photo was taken by photographer Linda McCartney, Paul's wife.

movements were simple, full of joy. For nearly ten years, de Kooning continued to work, even though he had symptoms of Alzheimer's, a disease that destroys the memory as it weakens the brain. As always, de Kooning had people talking. Some whispered that he was too sick to lift a brush, that his assistants were actually doing the new paintings for him.

A newspaper reporter decided to find out the truth. He visited de Kooning and Elaine on Long Island. At first he was sure the talkers were right. The man who met him at the door walked slowly, mumbled to himself, and could not remember what day it was.

But then Elaine asked de Kooning to show the reporter his new paintings. When they got inside the studio and de Kooning was in front of his work, he changed. He stood up straight. His mind and eyes were suddenly bright. He talked about each painting as if it were an old friend. The reporter said later that it was as if there were two de Koonings. De Kooning the man, he said, had begun to disappear. "But de Kooning the artist was still healthy."

Sadly, Elaine, who was a heavy smoker, died of lung cancer in 1989. By then, de Kooning's mind was so weakened by Alzheimer's that he did not understand what had happened. He stopped painting and spent his days quietly, cared for by his daughter, Lisa, and a team of doctors and nurses.

In the final year of his life, four major museums showed de Kooning's last paintings. The biggest exhibit, at the Museum of Modern Art, caused critics and visitors to disagree. Some said the paintings showed that de Kooning was a sick, confused old man when he did them. They missed the violence and swirling action of his early paintings. Others said these late works showed de Kooning had changed and grown as an artist. He had come to feel peaceful and calm.

While art lovers and critics were busy talking about de Kooning and his work, the artist was at home in bed. On March 13, 1997, just a few weeks before his ninety-third birthday, he died.

Even if he had lived longer, de Kooning probably would not have paid much attention to the fuss. All he had ever cared about was his work. "Paint," he had told Elaine years before, "as if every stroke is your last."

Timeline

1904   Born in Holland.

1926   Travels to America.

1927   Moves into an apartment in New York City.

1935-36 Finds work with the WPA Federal Art Project.

1942   Work is noticed and included in a gallery show.

1943   Marries Elaine Fried.

1948   Has first one-man art show.

1956   Daughter Lisa is born; separates from Elaine.

1962   Becomes an American citizen.

1963   Moves to Long Island and paints abstract landscapes.

1964   Receives Presidential Medal of Freedom.

1969   Travels to Japan and tries sculpture.

1978   Elaine returns; de Kooning stops drinking.

1989   Elaine dies; de Kooning stops painting.

1997   Four museums show latest work.

1997   Dies at home on March 13.

Words to Know

abstract—Art without familiar objects or people.

Abstract Expressionism—Artistic movement of the twentieth century that gave artists the freedom to paint emotions and attitudes. The pictures did not show realistic-looking objects.

Action Painting—Painting that shows brushstrokes and globs of paint, so that you can see the actions the artist took to create the work.

architect—Person who designs buildings.

canvas—Piece of stiff, stretched cloth to paint on.

critics—Experts who judge art.

Depression—A time in the 1930s when lots of Americans were without jobs and money.

distorted—Twisted, not normal.

Dutch—from Holland.

exhibition—Art show.

freighter—Boat that carries cargo, not people.

gallery—Place where art is hung and displayed.

Willem de Kooning

Internet Addresses

The best way to learn more about any artist, including Willem de Kooning, is to see the art—the real thing, not just photographs of it. That is easy if you happen to live in a large city with a large art museum, such as New York. But if you do not, try the Internet. The Web sites for de Kooning listed on the next page were written for people of all ages, so the text may be a bit too hard for you to get through. That is okay, though—you are just visiting for the pictures.

Abstract Expressionism You might want to learn more about the artistic movement called Abstract Expressionism that de Kooning was part of. You can also view a number of his paintings at this site.

http://arthistory.about.com/cs/abstractexpress

Online Museum Sites Another good site lists and links to all the online museum sites that have works by de Kooning that you can see.

http://www.artcyclopedia.com/artists/de_kooning_willem.html

Artnet Magazine has posted a review of the 1997 de Kooning show at the Metropolitan Museum of Art in New York. The review includes pictures of the works. Click on the small pictures to see larger versions.

http://www.artnet.com/Magazine/features/klein/klein2-14-97.asp

Index

DATE DUE